HAUNTED SHIPS AND LIGHTHOUSES

A Crabtree Branches Book

THOMAS KINGSLEY TROUPE

Crabtree Publishing
crabtreebooks.com

School-to-Home Support for Caregivers and Teachers

This high-interest book is designed to motivate striving students with engaging topics while building fluency, vocabulary, and an interest in reading. Here are a few questions and activities to help the reader build upon his or her comprehension skills.

Before Reading:

- *What do I think this book is about?*
- *What do I know about this topic?*
- *What do I want to learn about this topic?*
- *Why am I reading this book?*

During Reading:

- *I wonder why...*
- *I'm curious to know...*
- *How is this like something I already know?*
- *What have I learned so far?*

After Reading:

- *What was the author trying to teach me?*
- *What are some details?*
- *How did the photographs and captions help me understand more?*
- *Read the book again and look for the vocabulary words.*
- *What questions do I still have?*

Extension Activities:

- *What was your favorite part of the book? Write a paragraph on it.*
- *Draw a picture of your favorite thing you learned from the book.*

TABLE OF CONTENTS

SPOOKY SEAS

You stand on the main deck of the old ship, now permanently docked near the abandoned lighthouse. The wind howls across the harbor, carrying with it an unfamiliar voice. Icicles race down your spine as you thought you were alone. A light flickers in the towering lighthouse's small window. Are ghosts clinging to this ship and lighthouse?

Just about any place in the world can be haunted. Ships and lighthouses are places men and women of the sea spent years of their lives. It seems some aren't ready to leave...even after death.

Grab your flashlight and take a deep breath. You're about to discover why these ships and lighthouses are among...

THE HAUNTED.

FRIGHTENING FACT

There are more than 22,900 lighthouses around the world.

SS OURANG MEDAN, INDONESIA

The *SS Ourang Medan* was a cargo ship from Indonesia. In the late 1940s, it radioed for help while at sea. The message said everyone on the ship was likely dead. Another message simply said, "I die."

Rescue ships found the ship at sea with no one controlling it. Everyone on board was indeed dead, their faces frozen in terror.

There was no explanation as to what happened to the *Ourang Medan*. Some believed **paranormal** forces killed the entire crew. The rescue boats attempted to bring the cursed cargo ship back to land when a fire started below deck. As soon as they cut the tow cables, the *Ourang Medan* exploded and sank to the bottom of the sea. No one knows how the crew died or what caused the explosion.

U-BOAT 65, GERMANY

During World War I, Germany was building U-Boats to help them in battle. U-Boat 65 was tragic from the start. Many died during its construction. A military officer was killed when a torpedo exploded at sea.

Nearly everyone on the ship's crew saw the officer's ghost. The ghost would walk up the gangplank, look out at the sea then disappear.

FRIGHTENING FACT

In 1918, U-Boat 65 was spotted by an American submarine a few months before the war ended. Before the submarine could fire on the enemy, the U-Boat exploded on its own.

BELLE OF LOUISVILLE, KENTUCKY

The Belle of Louisville is a steam ship built in 1914. It served as a ferry, mail delivery boat, and an **excursion** vessel. The boat is considered a National Historic Landmark.

Shortly after World War II, Captain Ben Withers suffered a heart attack and died aboard the Belle. His ghost still haunts the boat as many have seen his image appear.

QUEEN MARY, LONG BEACH, CALIFORNIA

The *Queen Mary* is an ocean liner that was built in the 1930s. It was considered one of the grandest ships in the water. It carried Hollywood celebrities, royalty, and **dignitaries**.

It was docked for the last time as a passenger ship in September of 1939. It was later used to transport soldiers during World War II. During the war, the *Queen Mary* rammed into an escort ship causing the escort to sink.

FRIGHTENING FACT

The *Queen Mary* was repainted gray to serve as a troopship during World War II. Her nickname during this period was "Grey Ghost."

Like most haunted ships, the *Queen Mary* wasn't without tragedy. During its time as an ocean liner, 49 people died. Some consider the boat one of the most haunted places in the United States.

Investigators claim to have felt the presence of a firefighter who was crushed to death by a watertight door. Others believe the swimming pool is haunted by a young girl who drowned there.

The *Queen Mary* is no longer cruising the ocean. Instead, it's forever docked and was turned into a hotel. **Stateroom** B430 is considered the most haunted room on the ship. Faucets turn on by themselves, doors shut on their own, sheets will get pulled off while people sleep, and a dark figure will appear at the end of the bed. Stay there if you dare!

Talacre Point of Ayr Lighthouse, Wales

Along the north coast of Wales, the Talacre Point of Ayr Lighthouse stands tall. Built in 1776, it was used to guide ships entering the River Dee. It was abandoned in the 1840s, but apparently not completely.

At night, the ghost of a man in old-time clothes sometimes appears. He's been spotted at the top of the lighthouse, looking out over the sea.

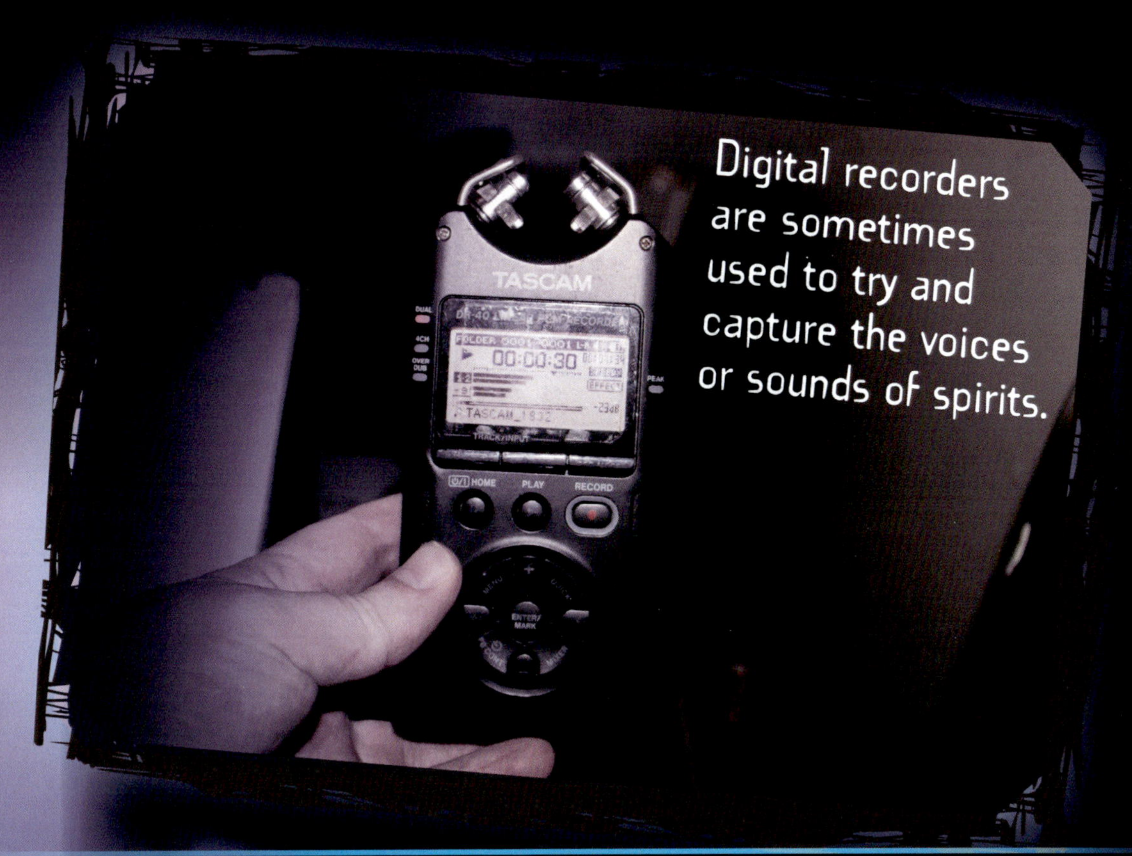

Digital recorders are sometimes used to try and capture the voices or sounds of spirits.

FRIGHTENING FACT

Paranormal investigators made contact with a spirit named Raymond while at the lighthouse. Raymond was a lighthouse keeper who died there from a fever.

POINT LOOKOUT LIGHTHOUSE, MARYLAND

The Point Lookout Lighthouse sits at the southern tip of St. Mary's County in Maryland. It was built in 1830 to guide boats along the Potomac River and Chesapeake Bay.

During the Civil War, a prisoner of war camp was built just north of the lighthouse. Around 4,000 men died and were buried there. The graves were later removed. Female prisoners were imprisoned and tortured at the lighthouse.

The lighthouse is no longer in use, but is still active. The spirit of a woman in a white **blouse** and a long blue dress appears at the top of the stairs. Some believe it is Pamelia Edwards, who was the lighthouse keeper during the Civil War.

Doors open and close on their own. People have heard snoring and voices whisper from the beyond.

A room on the upper level had a rotting smell and nothing could be done about the stink. **Parapsychologists** investigated and determined that it came from the pain and suffering from past prisoners held there. Soon after they made that statement, the smell was gone.

SOUTER LIGHTHOUSE, ENGLAND

The red and white striped Souter Lighthouse sits in Marsden, a village in England. Built in 1871, it was the first to use electricity to power its bright light. The lighthouse was **decommissioned** in 1988, but remains open for tours.

Lighthouse staff have seen spoons float, discovered cold spots, and felt something grab them. Most of the paranormal activity happens in the kitchen and living quarters.

FRIGHTENING FACT

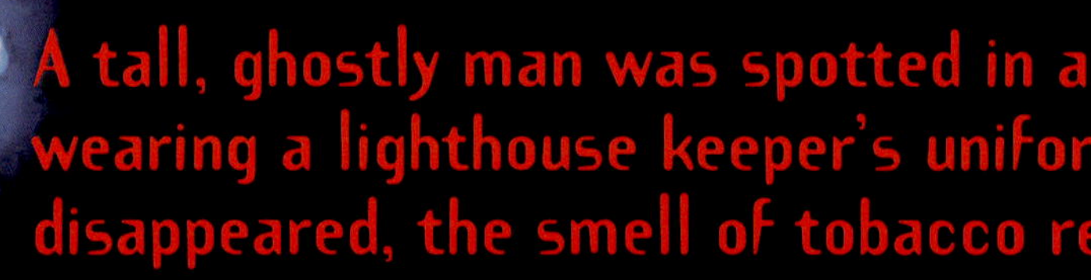

A tall, ghostly man was spotted in a hallway, wearing a lighthouse keeper's uniform. When he disappeared, the smell of tobacco remained.

POINT SUR LIGHTHOUSE, CALIFORNIA

The Point Sur Lighthouse in California looks out over the beautiful Pacific Ocean coastline. It was built in 1889 and was one of the most **remote** lighthouses in the country. The nearest doctor was four hours away and the nearest county road was a several-mile journey.

Families lived in and operated the lighthouse until it was **automated** in 1972.

It is believed the families that used to live in the lighthouse haunt the landmark to this day. Tour guides often call out to the ghosts, asking for permission to come inside. Some of the guides have captured voices on their recorders.

People have spotted ghosts on the property. One was a ghost of a man standing outside and looking into the living room window.

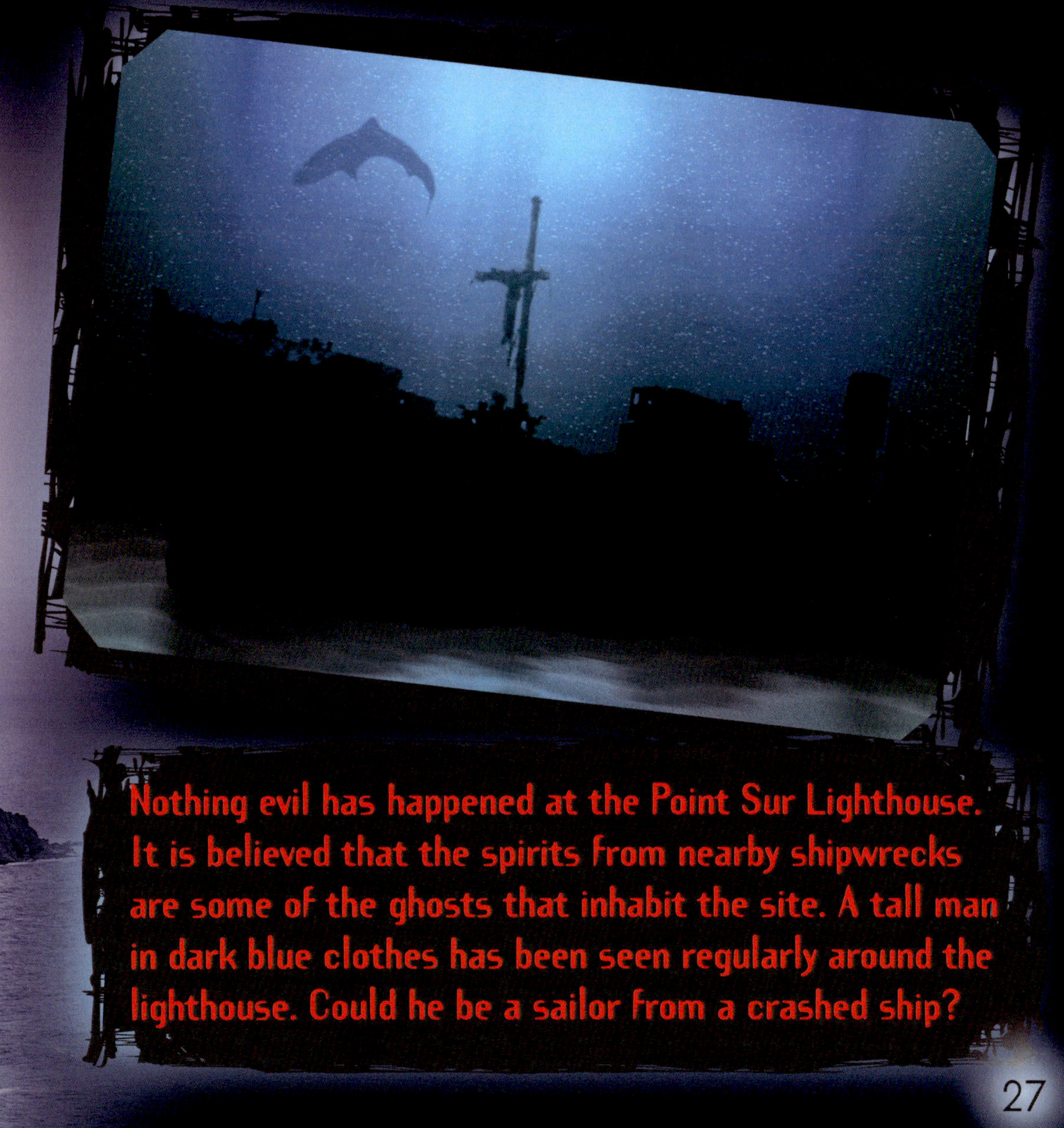

Nothing evil has happened at the Point Sur Lighthouse. It is believed that the spirits from nearby shipwrecks are some of the ghosts that inhabit the site. A tall man in dark blue clothes has been seen regularly around the lighthouse. Could he be a sailor from a crashed ship?

CONCLUSION

Do ghosts truly haunt these ships and lighthouses? What one person sees, another might explain away.

It's up to you to decide for yourself. If you hear or see something creepy, write it down or capture it with a camera. The evidence you discover might bring us closer to understanding...THE HAUNTED.

GLOSSARY

automated (aw-tuh-MAT-id): A system that works on its own without the help of a human

blouse (BLOUZ): A loose type of shirt usually worn by a woman

decommissioned (dee-kuhm-ISH-uhnd): Removed from service

dignitaries (DIG-nuh-tair-eez): Important people of high position

excursion (ek-SKUR-zhuhn): A brief trip for fun and pleasure

paranormal (pa-ruh-NOR-muhl): Strange events that are beyond normal understanding

parapsychologists (pa-ruh-sye-KOL-uh-jists): People who study paranormal events and the unexplainable

remote (ri-MOHT): Far away or distant

stateroom (STATE-room): A private room on a ship or a train

INDEX

WEBSITES TO VISIT

https://kids.kiddle.co/Ghost

www.hauntedrooms.co.uk/ghost-stories-kids-scary-childrens

ABOUT THE AUTHOR

Thomas Kingsley Troupe

Thomas Kingsley Troupe is the author of a whole pile of books for kids. He's written about ghosts, Bigfoot, werewolves, and even a book about dirt. When he's not writing or reading, he investigates the paranormal as part of the Twin Cities Paranormal Society. He lives in Woodbury, Minnesota with his 2 sons.

Crabtree Publishing

crabtreebooks.com 800-387-7650

Produced by: Blue Door Education for Crabtree Publishing
Written by: Thomas Kingsley Troupe
Designed by: Jennifer Dydyk
Edited by: Kelli Hicks
Proofreader: Crystal Sikkens
Production manager: Candice Campbell
Prepress technician: Katherine Kantor

Hardcover	978-1-4271-5559-7
Paperback	978-1-4271-5565-8
Ebook (pdf)	978-1-4271-5571-9
Epub	978-1-4271-5577-1
Read-along	978-1-4271-5583-2
Audio book	978-1-4271-5589-4

Printed in the U.S.A./072025/CP20250722

Published in Canada
Crabtree Publishing
616 Welland Avenue
St. Catharines, Ontario
L2M 5V6

Published in the United States
Crabtree Publishing
347 Fifth Avenue
Suite 1402-145
New York, NY 10016

The images/photos depicting "ghosts" in this book are artists' interpretations. The publisher does not claim these are actual images/photos taken of the ghosts mentioned in this book.

Photographs: Cover: lighthouse and captain © lassedesignen, ship deck © Tanya Sid, skull on cover and throughout book © Fer Gregory, pages 4-5 creepy picture borders here and throughout book © Dmitry Natashin, page 4 © Rush Photography Calgary, page 5 © Shi Yali, page 6 map © Intrepix, ship © Chris Iseli, page 7 © Joe Prachatree, pages 9 u-boat © Massimo Vernicesole, officer © Kozlik, page 10 © Thomas Kelley, page 12 © Editorial credit: Philip Pilosian / Shutterstock.com, page 15 © DarkBird, page 16 © hristianRogersPhotograph, page 17 © Juiced Up Media, pages 18-19 © Rhys Felsher, page 20 © AlessandraRC, page 21 g Daniel M. Silva, page 22 © JPMedia Productions, page 23 © Anthony McLaughlin, pages 24-25 © Rodrigo Sa Barreto, page 25 inset photo © Lynn Yeh, page 26 © travelview, page 27 © Grindi, page 28 © ArtMediaWorx, page 29 © Ashley EM. All images from Shutterstock.com except page 11 courtesy of the U.S. National Archives, page 13 courtesy of the U.S. Navy, page 14 © David Krieger https://creativecommons.org/licenses/by/2.0/deed.en

Library and Archives Canada Cataloguing in Publication

Title: Haunted ships and lighthouses / Thomas Kingsley Troupe.
Names: Troupe, Thomas Kingsley, author.
Description: Series statement: The haunted! | "A Crabtree branches book". | Includes index.
Identifiers: Canadiana (print) 20210220244 |
Canadiana (ebook) 20210220252 |
ISBN 9781427155597 (hardcover) |
ISBN 9781427155658 (softcover) |
ISBN 9781427155719 (HTML)
ISBN 9781427155771 (EPUB) |
ISBN 9781427155832 (read-along ebook)
Subjects: LCSH: Haunted places—Juvenile literature. | LCSH: Ships—Juvenile literature. | LCSH: Haunted lighthouses—Juvenile literature. | LCSH: Ghosts—Juvenile literature.
Classification: LCC BF1486 .T76 2022 | DDC j133.1/22—dc23

Library of Congress Cataloging-in-Publication Data

Names: Troupe, Thomas Kingsley, author.
Title: Haunted ships and lighthouses / Thomas Kingsley Troupe.
Description: New York, NY : Crabtree Publishing Company, [2022] | Series: The haunted! - a Crabtree Branches book | Includes index.
Identifiers: LCCN 2021022578 (print) | LCCN 2021022579 (ebook) |
ISBN 9781427155597 (hardcover) |
ISBN 9781427155658 (paperback) |
ISBN 9781427155719 (ebook) |
ISBN 9781427155771 (epub) |
ISBN 9781427155832
Subjects: LCSH: Haunted ships--Juvenile literature. | Haunted lighthouses--Juvenile literature. | Ghosts--Juvenile literature.
Classification: LCC BF1486 .T76 2022 (print) | LCC BF1486 (ebook) | DDC 133.1/2--dc23
LC record available at https://lccn.loc.gov/2021022578
LC ebook record available at https://lccn.loc.gov/2021022579